LACIE TART

Simple CRM Databases for Businesses on a Budget

How to Choose Software that Works for Your Business

Copyright © 2024 by Lacie Tart

All rights reserved. No part of this publication may be reproduced, stored or transmitted in any form or by any means, electronic, mechanical, photocopying, recording, scanning, or otherwise without written permission from the publisher. It is illegal to copy this book, post it to a website, or distribute it by any other means without permission.

First edition

This book was professionally typeset on Reedsy. Find out more at reedsy.com

Contents

	Introduction	1
1	Chapter 1: Why CRM Matters for Small Businesses	5
2	Chapter 2: Layout and Interface	22
3	Chapter 3: Functionality	27
4	Chapter 4: Reporting	33
5	Chapter 5: Integrations	37
6	Chapter 6: CRM Solutions To Consider	44
7	Chapter 7: Cost-Benefit Analysis and Key Tips for Success	49

Introduction

Choosing the Right CRM Database for Your Business

Running a successful small business means juggling a lot of moving parts—managing sales, marketing, customer service, and productivity all at once. It's no small task. For many business owners, finding the time and resources to stay organized and ensure customer satisfaction can feel like an uphill battle. That's where a Customer Relationship Management (CRM) system comes in. The right CRM software can help you keep track of customer interactions, streamline workflows, and boost your team's productivity—all while providing a consistent, high-quality experience for your customers.

But here's the catch: not all CRMs are created equal. Choosing the wrong one can lead to wasted time, frustrated employees, and money down the drain. In fact, studies show that of the 90% of CRM implementations that fail — the primary culprit is lack of user adoption. Even the most advanced software won't do your business any good if your team doesn't use it. That's why selecting a simple, user-friendly CRM that aligns with your team's needs and habits is crucial.

I am Lacie Tart. I have offered consulting on CRM software since 2007 and even before that if you count the Microsoft Access days. My first experience with CRM was with Goldmine in 2005, and since then I have become a certified ACT! Consultant and

Trainer, as well as a proficient user and trainer on various CRM platforms including Salesforce, Hubspot, Nimble, RedtailCRM for Financial Advisors. I have a passion for CRM customization and design, with an emphasis on understanding YOUR business processes to create the most optimized experience for increased user satisfaction. Database software has always been a first love of mine, and I wanted to take my years of experience and digest it into a guide for small businesses to reference when choosing the software that is right for their business.

This book is your guide to choosing the *right* CRM solution—one that fits your budget, meets your needs, and most importantly, gets used by your team. We'll walk you through the essential features to look for, from activity tracking and reporting to email and workflow integrations. You'll learn how to evaluate potential solutions, keep your team's experience in mind, and implement a system that enhances your business's productivity and profitability. This guide is designed to be the first step in approaching your new technology initiative - CRM database selection.

At its core, a CRM - also known as Customer Relationship Management software, is more than just a tool; it's a strategy. It's about organizing and optimizing the way your business interacts with customers. A good CRM helps you do the following:

- **Enhance Customer Satisfaction**: By tracking every touchpoint with your customers, you can ensure a consistent and personalized experience.
- **Boost Productivity**: Automate repetitive tasks and centralize information so your team can focus on what they do best.

- **Track and Report Performance**: Get a clear picture of what's working (and what's not) with robust reporting features.
- **Manage Sales Opportunities**: Stay on top of leads and close deals more effectively with tools designed to streamline the sales process.

For small business owners, a CRM is a game-changer. It helps you stay organized, make data-driven decisions, and free up time to focus on growing your business.

What to Expect from This Book

This book is designed to take the guesswork out of selecting and implementing a CRM system. Whether you're starting from scratch or looking to upgrade your current setup, you'll find practical advice, actionable steps, and real-world examples to guide you along the way.

Here's a quick overview of what we'll cover:

1. **Key Features to Look For**: Understand the must-have functionalities that make a CRM effective.
2. **User-Friendly Design**: Learn how to evaluate layout and interface to ensure your team feels comfortable using the system.
3. **Powerful Functionality**: Explore features like automation, reporting, and integrations that can supercharge your business operations.
4. **Evaluating Integrations**: Discover how to connect your CRM with other tools your team already uses, from email platforms to accounting software.

5. **Top CRM Solutions**: Get an overview of some of the best CRM options for small businesses, complete with pros, cons, and pricing insights.
6. **Cost-Benefit Analysis**: Learn how to weigh the costs of a CRM against the benefits it provides, ensuring you get the best value for your investment.

Start With the End in Mind

Choosing a CRM isn't just a software decision—it's a business decision. A well-implemented CRM can become the backbone of your operations, empowering your team to deliver better results and creating a foundation for sustainable growth. But to achieve these benefits, you need to approach the process with clarity and intention.

Throughout this book, we'll keep the focus on simplicity, practicality, and real-world application. By the end, you'll have the knowledge and tools to select a CRM solution that fits your business's unique needs and sets you up for long-term success. Let's get started.

1

Chapter 1: Why CRM Matters for Small Businesses

So Let's Start with the What and the Why!

Customer Relationship Management (CRM) in a nutshell is designed for managing interactions with current and potential customers. By implementing CRM effectively, small businesses can streamline processes, build customer loyalty, and ultimately grow revenue. This chapter will walk you through the core concepts and features of CRM systems, setting the foundation for building a system tailored to your business needs.

What is CRM?

At its core, CRM is a combination of practices, strategies, and technologies that businesses use to manage and analyze customer interactions and data throughout the customer life-cycle. More commonly recognized as database software, it is typically designed to be contact-centric. Although some customers prefer company-centric data, this does not truly capture the power of CRM because personal touch and interactions are made with people of companies, not the companies themselves. This is one of the true distinctions of a true CRM system. The goal is to improve customer relationships and foster long-term loyalty with key contacts who are your customers. CRM tools centralize customer information, automate workflows, and provide insights to help you make data-driven decisions.

Key Benefits of CRM Systems

For small businesses, a CRM system can:

- **Centralize Customer Data:** Keep all customer details, communication history, and transaction records in one accessible location.
- **Improve Communication:** Streamline customer interactions and ensure consistent messaging across your team.
- **Enhance Productivity:** Automate repetitive tasks, freeing up time for your team to focus on high-value activities.
- **Provide Actionable Insights:** Analyze customer behavior and sales trends to make informed decisions.
- **Boost Customer Satisfaction:** Personalize interactions based on a clear understanding of customer needs and preferences.

Core Features of CRM Systems

While CRM platforms vary in complexity, most systems share these fundamental features:

1. **Contact Management:** A CRM database stores customer details, such as names, addresses, emails, and phone

numbers. This feature ensures that your team can quickly access the information they need to serve your customers.
2. **Sales Tracking:** CRM tools help you monitor your sales pipeline, track leads, and record the status of ongoing deals. This visibility enables you to identify bottlenecks and optimize your sales process.
3. **Task and Calendar Management:** Stay on top of follow-ups, appointments, and deadlines with built-in scheduling tools. Notifications and reminders help ensure that no opportunities are missed.
4. **Email Integration:** Many CRM systems integrate with email platforms, allowing you to send, track, and analyze emails directly from the system. This feature is essential for managing email campaigns and individual correspondence.
5. **Reporting and Analytics:** Gain insights into sales performance, customer behavior, and team productivity with customizable dashboards and reports.
6. **Workflow Automation:** Automate repetitive tasks, such as sending follow-up emails or updating records, to improve efficiency and reduce manual errors.

Types of CRM Systems

There are three main types of CRM systems, each catering to different business needs:

1. **Operational CRM:** Focuses on automating sales, marketing, and service processes to improve efficiency.
2. **Analytical CRM:** Emphasizes data analysis to gain insights into customer behavior and trends.

3. **Collaborative CRM:** Facilitates communication between teams and with customers, ensuring a seamless experience across touch-points.

Below, I took some of the various industries and outlined how each specific type of CRM can benefit the primary initiatives they find important.

Operational CRMs are designed to streamline and automate customer-facing processes like sales, marketing, and service. They are particularly beneficial for industries where customer interactions are frequent and managing relationships is key. Here are some industries that gain significantly from an Operational CRM:

1. Retail and E-commerce

- Why? These industries need to track customer purchases, segment audiences for targeted marketing, and provide excellent customer support.
- Example Use Cases:
- Personalized email campaigns.
- Automated follow-ups for abandoned carts.
- Loyalty program management.

2. Hospitality and Travel

- Why? Hotels, airlines, and travel agencies rely on customer satisfaction and loyalty.
- Example Use Cases:
- Managing bookings and reservations.

- Personalizing travel packages based on customer preferences.
- Automating post-stay feedback requests.

3. Healthcare

- Why? Patient relationship management is crucial for appointment scheduling, follow-ups, and patient engagement.
- Example Use Cases:
- Appointment reminders and follow-ups.
- Patient history tracking for personalized care.
- Managing billing and insurance communication.

4. Financial Services

- Why? Banks, insurance companies, and investment firms need to build trust and provide timely, personalized services.
- Example Use Cases:
- Lead tracking for new accounts or loans.
- Automated reminders for payment due dates.
- Customer segmentation for targeted financial product offers.

5. Real Estate

- Why? Agents and firms need to manage client relationships and streamline deal pipelines.
- Example Use Cases:
- Tracking potential buyers and sellers.

- Automating follow-ups on property inquiries.
- Managing contracts and documents in a centralized system.

6. Telecommunications

- Why? High competition requires excellent customer service and retention strategies.
- Example Use Cases:
- Managing service requests and complaints.
- Up-selling or cross-selling additional services.
- Automating customer retention campaigns.

7. Education

- Why? Schools, universities, and training organizations need to engage students, alumni, and staff effectively.
- Example Use Cases:
- Managing student enrollment and inquiries.
- Tracking alumni for fundraising campaigns.
- Automating communications for events or deadlines.

8. Professional Services

- Why? Consulting firms, legal practices, and IT services need to build and maintain client relationships.
- Example Use Cases:
- Tracking client projects and deliverables.
- Automating reminders for billing and follow-ups.
- Managing client feedback for improved service delivery.

9. Nonprofits

- Why? Donor relationships and volunteer coordination are critical for success.
- Example Use Cases:
- Automating donation acknowledgments and receipts.
- Segmenting donors for targeted campaigns.
- Tracking volunteer schedules and participation.

10. Manufacturing and Distribution

- Why? These businesses often deal with B2B sales and need to manage large client bases efficiently.
- Example Use Cases:
- Managing customer orders and inquiries.
- Tracking sales pipelines for distributors.
- Automating marketing campaigns for product launches.

Key Focuses for Operational CRMs

Operational CRMs are ideal for businesses that:

- Have high volumes of customer interactions.
- Require automation to save time and reduce manual errors.
- Need tools to improve sales, marketing, and service processes.
- Focus on scaling their operations while maintaining quality customer experiences.

Analytical CRMs are designed to analyze customer data to provide actionable insights for decision-making. They are especially beneficial for industries where understanding customer behavior, trends, and preferences can lead to better strategic planning and decision-making. Here are industries that can make excellent use of an Analytical CRM:

1. Retail and E-commerce

- Why? These industries thrive on data-driven marketing and sales strategies.
- How Analytical CRMs Help:
- Customer segmentation for targeted promotions.
- Analyzing purchase patterns to predict future buying behavior.
- Optimizing inventory based on demand trends.

2. Financial Services

- Why? Banks, insurance firms, and investment companies rely heavily on customer data to mitigate risk and enhance service offerings.
- How Analytical CRMs Help:
- Credit risk analysis and fraud detection.
- Customer lifetime value (CLV) analysis.
- Predicting customer churn to design retention strategies.

3. Telecommunications

- Why? Telecom providers collect vast amounts of customer data and need to optimize customer retention and service offerings.

- How Analytical CRMs Help:
- Identifying high-value customers to prioritize retention.
- Cross-selling and up-selling based on usage data.
- Tracking network usage for targeted service improvements.

4. Healthcare

- Why? Hospitals and healthcare providers need to leverage patient data for better care and operational efficiency.
- How Analytical CRMs Help:
- Analyzing patient outcomes to improve treatment protocols.
- Identifying trends in patient demographics or conditions.
- Enhancing patient satisfaction by tracking service feedback.

5. Hospitality and Travel

- Why? Hotels, airlines, and travel agencies rely on personalized customer experiences to drive loyalty.
- How Analytical CRMs Help:
- Analyzing booking patterns to predict travel trends.
- Optimizing pricing strategies through demand forecasting.
- Evaluating customer reviews for operational improvements.

6. Education

- Why? Schools, universities, and online education platforms need insights into enrollment trends and student engagement.
- How Analytical CRMs Help:
- Tracking student performance and engagement data.

- Analyzing enrollment trends to refine marketing efforts.
- Identifying at-risk students for targeted intervention.

7. Real Estate

- Why? Real estate agencies and property developers rely on market and client data for sales and investment strategies.
- How Analytical CRMs Help:
- Tracking buyer preferences to predict demand for property types.
- Analyzing market trends to guide pricing strategies.
- Identifying potential investment opportunities based on historical data.

8. Nonprofits

- Why? Donor insights and engagement analysis are crucial for sustainable fundraising.
- How Analytical CRMs Help:
- Analyzing donor giving patterns to improve campaigns.
- Identifying high-potential donors for personalized outreach.
- Measuring the effectiveness of fundraising strategies.

9. Manufacturing and Distribution

- Why? These businesses need insights into B2B customer trends and supply chain efficiency.
- How Analytical CRMs Help:
- Forecasting demand based on historical sales data.
- Identifying under-performing territories or accounts.

- Optimizing production schedules to meet customer demand.

10. Media and Entertainment

- Why? Media companies rely on audience insights for content strategy and ad sales.
- How Analytical CRMs Help:
- Tracking viewership or subscriber behavior to refine offerings.
- Analyzing advertising performance for optimization.
- Predicting trends to guide content creation.

Key Focuses for Analytical CRM

Analytical CRMs are especially suited for organizations:

- Operating in data-intensive environments.
- Needing deep customer behavior insights to make informed decisions.
- Prioritizing long-term customer retention and strategic planning.

Collaborative CRMs are designed to enhance communication and information sharing between teams and with external stakeholders (e.g., customers, suppliers, and partners). These systems are especially beneficial for industries where seamless collaboration and a unified view of customer interactions are essential. Here are some industries that benefit significantly from Collaborative CRMs:

1. Healthcare

- Why? Healthcare providers need to share patient information between doctors, nurses, specialists, and administrative staff.
- How Collaborative CRMs Help:
- Centralizing patient records to streamline care coordination.
- Enabling communication between departments for improved patient outcomes.
- Managing referrals and follow-ups seamlessly.

2. Real Estate

- Why? Agents, brokers, and support staff must collaborate to close deals efficiently.
- How Collaborative CRMs Help:
- Sharing client preferences and property information in real-time.
- Coordinating showings, offers, and negotiations among team members.
- Managing interactions with buyers, sellers, and service providers (e.g., inspectors, mortgage brokers).

3. Retail and E-commerce

- Why? Teams in sales, customer service, and marketing need to align to provide excellent customer experiences.
- How Collaborative CRMs Help:
- Coordinating customer interactions across online and offline channels.

- Sharing insights from customer service teams with marketing for tailored campaigns.
- Ensuring consistent messaging and promotions across teams.

4. *Manufacturing and Supply Chain*

- Why? Manufacturers rely on collaboration with distributors, suppliers, and customers to maintain efficiency.
- How Collaborative CRMs Help:
- Managing communications with suppliers and distributors to ensure smooth operations.
- Sharing customer feedback with production teams to improve products.
- Coordinating with sales teams to meet delivery timelines.

5. *Telecommunications*

- Why? Telecom companies need to align sales, support, and technical teams to ensure a seamless customer experience.
- How Collaborative CRMs Help:
- Enabling service teams to access customer history for efficient issue resolution.
- Sharing usage data with sales teams to recommend relevant upgrades.
- Streamlining communication between field technicians and customer service.

6. Education

- Why? Schools, universities, and training organizations require collaboration between faculty, administrative staff, and students.
- How Collaborative CRMs Help:
- Sharing student performance and engagement data among teachers and counselors.
- Coordinating with alumni for fundraising or mentorship programs.
- Facilitating communication between departments for enrollment and scheduling.

7. Nonprofits

- Why? Nonprofits often work with donors, volunteers, and staff across multiple locations.
- How Collaborative CRMs Help:
- Tracking donor communications and sharing updates across fundraising teams.
- Coordinating volunteer schedules and activities in real-time.
- Collaborating with external stakeholders, such as grant agencies or sponsors.

8. Travel and Hospitality

- Why? Travel agencies, hotels, and airlines need to provide consistent customer experiences across teams and locations.
- How Collaborative CRMs Help:

- Sharing customer preferences with staff across multiple properties or departments.
- Coordinating trip planning and booking details among travel agents.
- Managing communication with external partners, like tour operators or car rental companies.

9. Financial Services

- Why? Banks, insurance companies, and investment firms rely on team collaboration for customer on-boarding and service.
- How Collaborative CRMs Help:
- Sharing customer profiles between sales and service teams for a seamless experience.
- Enabling cross-functional teams to align on high-value client management.
- Improving coordination between branches and central offices.

10. Media and Entertainment

- Why? Collaboration between creative teams, advertisers, and customers is critical for success.
- How Collaborative CRMs Help:
- Coordinating projects between content creators, advertisers, and sales teams.
- Sharing audience insights to guide programming or advertising strategies.
- Streamlining interactions with external partners and agencies.

Key Focuses for Collaborative CRM

Collaborative CRMs are ideal for organizations that:

- Have multiple customer touch-points across teams or locations.
- Require consistent and seamless communication internally and externally.
- Serve customers or partners through complex, multi-step processes.

As you can see, most industry segments need all of these key initiatives to be successful. When choosing a CRM, pay attention to the software that gives you the MOST feature rich options for ALL of these three main types. This way you can prevent having to switch to another CRM solution later once your business scales and your needs evolve.

Choosing the Right CRM for Your Business

When selecting a CRM system, consider these factors:

- **Business Needs:** Identify the features most important to your operations.
- **Budget:** Look for affordable options that provide the functionality you need without unnecessary extras.
- **Ease of Use:** Choose a system that's intuitive for your team to adopt and use effectively.
- **Scalability:** Ensure the system can grow with your business.
- **Integration:** Confirm compatibility with existing tools, such as email or accounting software.

Conclusion

Understanding the basics of CRM is essential for building a system that works for your business. By familiarizing yourself with the key benefits, features, and types of CRM systems, you can make informed decisions and set the stage for long-term success. In the next chapter, we will explore how to assess your business's unique requirements AND explore what CRM options will most fit the working style and technology environment your team is currently using.

2

Chapter 2: Layout and Interface

When selecting a CRM solution, the layout and interface are the _MOST critical factors_ that significantly impact usability and adoption. A familiar and user-friendly interface encourages exploration and reduces the fear of engaging with new technology. This chapter will guide you on choosing a CRM system with an intuitive design, aesthetic appeal, and seamless integration with tools you already use.

The Importance of a Familiar Graphic User Interface (GUI)

For small business owners, navigating a CRM system should feel natural. A well-designed layouts and interfaces reduce the learning curve, allowing users to hover, search, and explore with confidence. Here are key characteristics of an effective CRM layout:

- **Simplicity:** Avoid systems cluttered with unnecessary features. Opt for a clean, minimalist design where essential tools are easy to locate.

- **Consistency:** A consistent layout ensures users can predict where to find features, building familiarity quickly.
- **Intuitiveness:** Choose a CRM that uses recognizable icons, straightforward labels, and a logical menu structure. If your team is comfortable with applications like Microsoft Excel or Google Workspace, look for similar interface elements in the CRM.

Aesthetics Matter

While functionality is crucial, the visual appeal of your CRM system should not be overlooked. A pleasant and modern design fosters a positive experience and encourages regular use. Look for:

- **Customizable Themes:** The ability to adjust colors, fonts, and layouts to match your brand or personal preferences.
- **Responsive Design:** Ensure the interface works seamlessly across devices, including desktops, tablets, and smartphones.
- **Visual Clarity:** Crisp typography, ample spacing, and clearly defined sections contribute to a user-friendly experience.

Integration with Existing Tools

Your CRM system should complement the software you already rely on. Seamless integration reduces workflow disruptions and ensures that data flows smoothly between platforms. Consider the following integrations when making your selection:

- **Email Platforms:** Ensure compatibility with Gmail, Outlook,

or other email clients for tracking communication.
- **Productivity Suites:** Look for integration with tools like Google Docs, Google Calendar, Microsoft Office, or Teams.
- **Accounting Software:** QuickBooks or similar tools should sync effortlessly with your CRM to manage invoicing and financial data.
- **Social Media:** Many CRMs offer features to monitor and engage with social media platforms like Facebook, Instagram, and LinkedIn.
- **E-commerce Platforms:** If applicable, check for compatibility with platforms like Shopify or WooCommerce.

Integrations are included in the layout and interface section of this book because how the integrations convey in your CRM is a very important aspect of workflow. Does your integrated software show up as a primary design of your CRM, or do you have to maneuver through space and time to find it? Is it part of the design workflow for the CRM and conceptualized as a cohesive part of the overall picture, or does your integrated software feel like an outsider to the main idea? Keep this in mind when choosing a CRM for it's integration. If you can't find it, locate it or access it easily, will you even use it? Probably not.

Customization and Flexibility

No two businesses are the same, and your CRM should reflect that. Customization options allow you to tailor the system to your unique workflows and preferences. However, it is important to avoid overloading the system with excessive customizations that users may not adopt. Stick to adjustments that enhance usability and support your team's core tasks. Features to look for include:

- **Custom Fields:** Add fields to track information specific to your business.
- **Adjustable Dashboards:** Personalize dashboards to display the metrics and reports most relevant to your goals.
- **Role-Based Permissions:** Set up access levels to ensure team members see only the data they need.
- **Automation Settings:** Fine-tune workflows to match your processes, such as automated follow-ups or data entry.

PRO Tip: Try to avoid removing core fields from your database that come with the original design. These fields are tried and true and often have relationships with data you will need to report on. It's ok to add a field, but be careful what you take away. If you don't want to see a field, simply remove it from the layout.

Tips for Evaluating CRM Layouts

- **Request a Demo:** Most CRM providers offer free demos or trials. Use this opportunity to explore the interface and test its usability.
- **Seek Feedback:** Involve your team in evaluating potential systems. Their input is invaluable for understanding usability from different perspectives.
- **Test and Preview Integrations:** During the trial, test integrations with your existing tools to ensure smooth functionality.

Conclusion

Choosing a CRM system with an intuitive layout and interface is essential for ensuring adoption and effectiveness. Prioritize familiarity, aesthetic appeal, and seamless integration with your existing software ecosystem. By selecting a CRM that feels like a natural extension of your current tools, you'll empower your team to embrace the technology and maximize its potential. The next chapter will focus on assessing your business needs to create a CRM implementation strategy tailored to your goals.

3

Chapter 3: Functionality

When evaluating a CRM system, *functionality is at the heart of its value*. A solution must cater to different learning styles, streamline processes, and encourage natural adoption through smart features and intuitive design. This chapter explores key functionalities that make a CRM effective and user-friendly, ensuring your team can perform tasks efficiently and with minimal friction.

Adapting to Different Learners

A great CRM system provides multiple ways to accomplish the same task, accommodating diverse learning styles and preferences. For instance:

- **Visual Learners:** Dashboards with visual cues such as charts and graphs make data easy to understand.
- **Hands-On Learners:** Interactive guides or drag-and-drop features facilitate engagement.
- **Text-Oriented Learners:** Detailed menus and help articles

offer clarity for users who prefer written instructions.

By offering flexibility, a CRM ensures that every team member can use the system comfortably and effectively.

Reducing Unnecessary Clicks

Efficiency is essential in a well-designed CRM. The system should minimize the number of steps required to complete tasks, avoiding unnecessary clicks or complicated workflows. Look for features like:

- **Quick Action Buttons:** Enable one-click access to commonly used tools or functions.
- **Custom Shortcuts:** Allow users to create personalized shortcuts for frequent actions.
- **Streamlined Navigation:** Ensure menus and features are logically organized, reducing time spent searching for options.

Encouraging Natural Adoption

Adoption is a key challenge when introducing new software. Databases with smart features that simplify tasks and anticipate user needs can foster natural adoption. Examples include:

- **Auto-Population of Data:** Automatically fill in details using integrations with social media or databases, reducing manual entry.
- **Predictive Insights:** Suggest next steps based on historical data and user behavior.

- **Automation:** Automatically schedule follow-ups, send reminders, or generate reports, freeing users to focus on strategic activities.

Intuitive Design for Workflow Optimization

An intuitive CRM design aligns with your team's natural workflow, making it clear what actions to take next. Key considerations include:

- **Logical Sequencing:** Features and options should appear in the order they are typically used.
- **Clear Labels:** Use straightforward terminology to guide users effectively.
- **Contextual Help:** Provide tips or guidance within the interface when users need it most.

PRO Tip:
Things to note when choosing a database software with the ability to create custom fields is that planning for the most effective use of the data is PARAMOUNT. Research and investigate what data you will ACTUALLY use instead of data you think you will use for customizing your database. Remember less is more. Distinct fields are important for reporting purposes ONLY. If you create fields that are ambiguous, aren't fields you will need to report on, or fields your users will not utilize, you have created another task for the user to do. It's important to capture the data that is most meaningful and NOT a bunch of meaningless data. Keep in mind that you can limit what your users see by creating custom layouts for specific users and departments. Your goal is to create a tool that users love and not to burden your team and hinder productivity and success. If you

need help, hire a certified CRM consultant that can help you plan in strategic ways and who can help you ask the right questions.

Core Functionalities of an Effective CRM

To maximize productivity and customer satisfaction, ensure your CRM includes these critical features:

1. Salesforce Automation

Streamline your sales process with tools to:

- Track leads and manage the sales pipeline.
- Automate repetitive tasks like follow-up emails.
- Provide visibility into deal progress with real-time updates.

2. Customer Service & Support

Enhance the customer experience with:

- A centralized ticketing system to manage inquiries.
- Knowledge bases for self-service options.
- Tools to track resolution times and customer satisfaction metrics.

3. Marketing Automation

Improve outreach efforts through:

- Campaign management tools to plan and execute marketing initiatives.
- Segmentation features to target specific customer groups.
- Analytics to measure campaign effectiveness and ROI.

4. CRM Project Management

Integrate project management features to:

- Collaborate on tasks and projects within the CRM.
- Assign responsibilities and track progress.
- Link projects to customer records for better context.

5. Social CRM

Leverage social media integrations to:

- Monitor brand mentions and customer feedback.
- Engage with customers directly from the CRM.
- Gain insights into customer preferences and behavior.

Conclusion

Functionality is the backbone of any CRM system. By selecting a solution that supports diverse learners, reduces friction, and integrates seamlessly into workflows, you can ensure high adoption rates and productivity. Prioritize smart features, intuitive design, and comprehensive tools to empower your team and enhance customer relationships. The next chapter will delve into implementing a CRM system tailored to your business needs.

4

Chapter 4: Reporting

One of the most powerful aspects of a CRM system is its ability to provide visibility into the bigger picture of your business operations. Reporting tools and dashboards offer management the insights needed to understand what is and is not being done, driving accountability, analysis, and productivity improvements. This chapter explores how to harness CRM reporting features to keep your team on track and your business growing.

Seeing the Bigger Picture

Effective reporting bridges the gap between day-to-day operations and long-term strategy. By analyzing trends and patterns, CRM reports help management:

- **Identify Gaps:** Spot incomplete tasks, overlooked opportunities, or areas that require more attention.
- **Monitor Performance:** Track individual, team, and departmental productivity.

- **Set Benchmarks:** Use historical data to establish realistic goals and expectations.

Dashboards: Real-Time Accountability

Dashboards provide a snapshot of your key metrics at a glance, making it easy to monitor progress in real time. A well-designed CRM dashboard should include:

- **Customizable Widgets:** Allowing users to display the most relevant metrics for their role.
- **Visual Indicators:** Graphs, charts, and heat-maps that highlight trends and outliers.
- **Real-Time Updates:** Ensuring data is current, enabling quick decisions based on the latest information.

Dashboards empower your team by making performance transparent and fostering a culture of accountability. When everyone understands how their contributions impact the bigger picture, collaboration and focus improve.

Key Metrics for Analysis and Productivity

To truly benefit from CRM reporting, focus on metrics that provide actionable insights. Here are some examples:

Sales Metrics

- **Pipeline Velocity:** How quickly deals move through your sales funnel.
- **Conversion Rates:** The percentage of leads that turn into

paying customers.
- **Revenue by Source:** Identifying which channels or campaigns are driving the most revenue.

Customer Service Metrics

- **Resolution Time:** Average time to resolve customer inquiries.
- **Customer Satisfaction (CSAT):** Feedback on service quality.
- **First-Contact Resolution:** Percentage of issues resolved without requiring follow-ups.

Productivity Metrics

- **Task Completion Rates:** Percentage of assigned tasks completed on time.
- **Activity Tracking:** Number of calls, emails, or meetings logged by each team member.
- **Utilization Rates:** How effectively team members are using their time.

Reporting for Continuous Improvement

Reports should not just document past performance but also guide future actions. Use CRM reporting to:

- **Identify Trends:** Detect patterns in customer behavior, market conditions, or team performance.
- **Refine Strategies:** Adjust marketing campaigns, sales approaches, or service protocols based on data insights.
- **Promote Accountability:** Share reports regularly with your

team to ensure transparency and alignment.

Avoiding Reporting Overload

While comprehensive reporting is valuable, it's important to avoid overloading your team with excessive or irrelevant data. This goes hand and hand with creating customized fields. Follow these guidelines when determining what data you want to report on:

- **Focus on Key Metrics:** Choose a handful of meaningful indicators that align with your goals.
- **Automate Reports:** Schedule regular reports to be generated and shared automatically.
- **Simplify Visuals:** Use clear, concise visualizations to make data easy to interpret.

Conclusion

Reporting is a cornerstone of effective CRM use, enabling management to see what is working, what needs attention, and how to optimize for success. By leveraging dashboards and tailored metrics, you can foster personal responsibility, drive analysis, and improve productivity across your team. In the next chapter, we will dive into exploring the most commonly used integrations that transform your technology into a system that works cohesively for maximum impact and results. The right integrations can take your business to the next level because data will work in more powerful ways and produce deeper insights. This can and should also create a more meaningful customer experience.

5

Chapter 5: Integrations

Supercharging Your CRM with Smart Integrations

Imagine your CRM as the hub of your business operations. It's powerful on its own, but its real strength comes from the connections it can make. With the right integrations, your CRM evolves into a productivity powerhouse, streamlining workflows and reducing the need for constant toggling between platforms. The key? Choosing integrations that truly work *with* your CRM—not just beside it. Let's explore how to harness these tools and supercharge your CRM.

What Makes a Great Integration?

Before diving into specific integrations, it's essential to understand what separates a good integration from a bad one. A great integration feels seamless: data flows effortlessly between your CRM and the external software, enabling automation and reducing manual work. Beware of integrations that merely provide a window into the other platform; they might look connected, but they won't deliver the productivity boost you're looking for.

Here's the litmus test: If an integration saves you time, reduces errors, and provides actionable insights, it's worth considering.

The Most Powerful CRM Integrations for Small Businesses

1. Email Marketing Integrations

Your CRM and email marketing platform should be best friends. Together, they help you nurture leads, automate campaigns, and track engagement. Look for integrations with popular platforms like:

- **Mailchimp**: Sync customer data to create targeted email campaigns and track their performance directly in your CRM.
- **Swiftpage**: Leverage email marketing and drip-marketing campaigns, landing pages and reporting analytics to update customer records and optimize lead-generation efforts.

2. Accounting Software

Integrating your accounting software with your CRM bridges the gap between sales and finance, providing a clearer picture of customer profitability. Some top options include:

- **QuickBooks**: Sync invoices, payments, and customer financial details for real-time visibility.

- **Xero**: Automate recurring invoicing and gain instant access to payment histories.

3. Social Media Platforms

Your CRM should be plugged into the platforms where your customers spend their time. Popular integrations include:

- **Instagram & Facebook**: Track ad performance and engagement metrics directly in your CRM.
- **LinkedIn**: Automatically capture lead data from LinkedIn ads or profiles, keeping your database fresh and accurate.

4. Communication and Collaboration Tools

Streamlining internal communication can skyrocket team productivity. Key integrations include:

- **Slack**: Receive CRM notifications directly in Slack channels for immediate action.
- **Project Management Tools**: Sync with platforms like Trello or Asana to connect customer data to project tasks.

5. Productivity Suites

Documents and spreadsheets are still integral to business operations. Integrating these tools ensures your data stays updated and accessible:

- **Google Workspace (Docs, Sheets)**: Automatically generate and update documents with CRM data.

- **Microsoft 365**: Create and share presentations or reports using live CRM data.

6. Mapping Software

For businesses with location-based needs, mapping integrations provide invaluable insights:

- **Google Maps**: Plan routes and visualize customer locations.
- **Yahoo Maps**: Compare traffic data and optimize travel times.

7. Automation Platforms

When your CRM can't integrate natively, platforms like these step in to fill the gap:

- **Zapier**: Connect your CRM with thousands of apps for automated workflows.
- **Integrately**: A cost-effective alternative for building custom workflows.

8. Calendar and Scheduling

Simplify meeting management with integrations that sync schedules seamlessly:

- **Google Calendar**: Schedule calls and appointments directly from your CRM.
- **Microsoft Outlook**: Link email and calendar for smoother follow-ups.

9. E-Commerce Platforms

For businesses in retail or online sales, these integrations provide a complete view of customer purchases:

- **Shopify**: Sync customer purchase history and automate personalized follow-ups.
- **WooCommerce**: Track order status and inventory directly in your CRM.

10. ERP Integrations

Enterprise Resource Planning (ERP) integrations connect your CRM to the broader business ecosystem, ensuring a unified data flow:

- Examples: NetSuite, Odoo

11. Document Automation

Streamline proposal and document creation with tools that pull data directly from your CRM:

- **PandaDoc**: Automate contracts, proposals, and agreements.
- **Proposify**: Generate professional documents tailored to your client's needs.

12. Analytics and Reporting

Insights are only as good as the data you're analyzing. Boost your CRM's analytics capabilities with these integrations:

- **Google Analytics**: Tie website traffic and conversion data to CRM records.
- **Tableau**: Create advanced, visually rich reports from CRM data.

Key Considerations for Choosing Integrations

When evaluating integrations, keep these questions in mind:

1. **Will it save time?** Look for features that automate repetitive tasks.
2. **Does it reduce errors?** Ensure data synchronization is accurate and reliable.
3. **Is it scalable?** Choose integrations that grow with your business needs.
4. **What's the cost?** Consider the return on investment in terms of saved time and increased productivity.

Bringing It All Together

Integrations transform your CRM from a standalone tool into a central nervous system for your business. By thoughtfully connecting the platforms you rely on, you'll streamline processes, enhance efficiency, and unlock new opportunities for growth. Start by identifying your biggest time sinks and productivity bottlenecks, and prioritize integrations that directly address those challenges. With the right integrations in place, your CRM won't just work with your business; it will work *for it*, driving you toward greater success.

6

Chapter 6: CRM Solutions To Consider

Finding the Right CRM for Your Business

Choosing the right CRM is like picking the perfect pair of shoes—it needs to fit your needs, your budget, and your team. With so many options on the market, it's easy to feel overwhelmed. But here's the good news: you don't need enterprise-grade software designed for massive corporations. For small businesses, there are plenty of affordable and user-friendly options that pack a punch without overwhelming you with features you'll never use. Let's take a closer look at seven standout CRM solutions tailored to small businesses and even sole proprietors.

1. ***Nimble CRM***

If you're looking for a CRM that combines simplicity with power, Nimble deserves your attention. It's particularly well-suited for small teams or even solo entrepreneurs who need an intuitive way to manage relationships and sales. Nimble excels at integrating seamlessly with email platforms and social media, allowing you to track conversations and engagement across multiple channels. Its clean interface and smart contact management tools make it a joy to use without requiring a steep learning curve.

Highlights:

- Social media integration for a complete view of customer interactions.
- Email syncing to keep conversations organized.
- Affordable pricing plans designed for small businesses.

2. *Zoho CRM*

Zoho CRM has earned a strong reputation as an all-in-one solution for small businesses. Its flexibility allows you to customize workflows and dashboards to suit your needs. Whether you're managing a sales pipeline or tracking marketing campaigns, Zoho provides a solid foundation without breaking the bank. Its pricing plans scale well, offering advanced features as your business grows.

Highlights:

- Highly customizable workflows and reporting tools.
- Integration with Zoho's suite of business apps.
- Affordable entry-level pricing for small teams.

3. *ACT! CRM*

ACT! CRM is a classic choice that has evolved over the years to remain relevant. Designed with small businesses in mind, it combines robust contact management with marketing automation features. While its interface might feel a bit dated compared to newer solutions, it delivers solid functionality where it counts.

Highlights:

- Strong contact and opportunity management.
- Built-in marketing automation.
- Scalable options for growing businesses.

4. *SugarCRM*

For businesses that need a bit more flexibility and don't mind some technical customization, SugarCRM is worth a look. This open-source platform offers a range of tools for sales, marketing, and customer service. It's a step up in complexity compared to simpler options but provides the scalability that many small businesses need.

Highlights:

- Open-source flexibility for custom integrations.
- Comprehensive tools for sales and customer support.
- Suitable for small businesses with growing needs.

5. *Microsoft Dynamics 365 CRM*

While Microsoft Dynamics has an enterprise-grade reputation, its CRM solutions also cater to small businesses. It's particularly valuable if you're already using Microsoft 365 tools, as the integration is seamless. From tracking sales leads to managing customer service, Microsoft Dynamics offers robust functionality in a familiar ecosystem.

Highlights:

- Deep integration with Microsoft 365.
- Scalable plans for small businesses.
- Reliable and secure infrastructure.

6. *Hubspot CRM*

HubSpot is an excellent choice for small businesses because it offers a free, easy-to-use CRM that provides essential tools for managing sales, marketing, and customer service in one platform. It's scalable, allowing businesses to start with the free plan and add advanced features as they grow. HubSpot's intuitive interface, automation capabilities, and integration with popular apps make it accessible for small teams to improve efficiency, streamline workflows, and enhance customer relationships without a steep learning curve or upfront investment.

Highlights:

- All-in-one platform
- User-friendly free plan
- Scalable with powerful integrations

7. *Salesforce.com*

Salesforce is a great choice for small to medium-sized businesses (SMBs) because it provides a highly customizable and scalable CRM platform that grows with the business. Salesforce empowers SMBs with enterprise-level capabilities to improve efficiency, boost sales, and deliver excellent customer experiences.

Highlights:

- Comprehensive and highly scalable
- Automation and AI features
- Extensive integrations and a deep user community for support and training

Bonus: Options for Sole Proprietors

If you're running a one-person operation, you need a CRM that's lightweight, affordable, and easy to use. Here are a couple of standout options:

- **Insightly**: Perfect for individuals who need project management alongside CRM functionality. It's simple, affordable, and designed for sole proprietors.
- **HubSpot CRM (Free Tier)**: HubSpot's free CRM provides a robust set of tools for individuals, including email tracking, deal management, and reporting.

Which CRM is Right for You?

This is not an exhaustive list, rather this list includes some of the most utilized, industry tested and standardized CRM solutions. Many of these have been around for a long time and are tried and tested. Don't be afraid to try new CRM technologies, but make sure they pass the litmus test that the old reliable systems have experience and expertise in as industry leaders. Each of these solutions has its strengths, and the best choice depends on your business's specific needs. Nimble stands out for its simplicity and social media integration, making it a great option for relationship-focused businesses. Zoho's customizability and affordability make it an excellent all-around choice, while options like Insightly cater specifically to solo entrepreneurs.

Take advantage of free trials and demos to test-drive these solutions before committing. The right CRM should feel like an extension of your business, making your work easier and your customer relationships stronger. In the next chapter, we will dive into strategies for training your team to make the most of your CRM system and preparing your cost benefits analysis.

7

Chapter 7: Cost-Benefit Analysis and Key Tips for Success

Balancing Cost with Value

Investing in a CRM is about finding the sweet spot where cost meets functionality. While some solutions may seem more expensive upfront, they often deliver the same—or even greater—value through advanced features, scalability, and better customer support. Understanding how to evaluate these costs and benefits is crucial for making an informed decision.

Comparing Costs vs. Benefits

When analyzing CRM options, don't just look at the price tag; consider what you're getting in return. Here are some factors to weigh:

1. **Features Included**: Does the CRM offer essential tools like automation, integrations, and analytics? Are those

features standard, or will you need to pay extra?
2. **Scalability**: Can the CRM grow with your business? Many solutions offer tiered pricing, so evaluate what's included at each level.
3. **Support**: Quality customer support can save hours of frustration. Is it included in the cost, or is it an add-on?
4. **User Experience**: A more intuitive CRM may require less training, reducing costs associated with on-boarding.

Example Cost-Benefit Breakdown

- **Low-Cost CRM**: Offers basic functionality but may lack integrations or automation, requiring manual work.
- **Mid-Tier CRM**: Higher cost, but includes features like email marketing integration, social media tracking, and robust reporting.
- **High-End CRM**: Top-tier features, extensive customization, and premium support. Higher price, but it's often worth it for businesses with complex needs.

Remember, the cheapest option isn't always the most cost-effective in the long run. A CRM that improves efficiency and enhances customer relationships will pay for itself through increased productivity and revenue.

Need to save time? Check out https://www.trustradius.com/compare-products for a comparison of the most commonly used and reviews for CRM software.

Tips for Optimizing Adoption and Success

1. Invest in Training

A CRM is only as good as the people using it. To maximize its value, prioritize training:

- **Individual and Group Training**: Many experts and providers offer courses tailored to specific CRMs. These can help your team unlock advanced features and improve their workflows.
- **Continuous Learning**: Schedule regular refresher sessions to keep users up to date as new features are rolled out.
- **Mandatory Continuing Education (CE)**: Implement a CE policy for your team to ensure consistent improvement in CRM usage.

2. Incentivize Engagement

Motivating your team to embrace the CRM can accelerate adoption. Here's how:

- **Rewards for Progress**: Offer gift cards, cash bonuses, or public recognition for users who demonstrate significant progress or commitment.
- **Super Users as Mentors**: Appoint power users to guide and support those struggling to adapt. This peer-driven approach fosters collaboration and reduces resistance to change.

3. Leverage Technology Updates

CRMs evolve rapidly, with new features designed to improve efficiency and productivity. Stay ahead by:

- **Embracing Updates**: Train your team to take full advantage of new tools and integrations as they become available.
- **Feedback Loops**: Encourage users to provide feedback on what's working and what isn't. Use this input to refine training and processes.

4. Set Clear Goals and Metrics

Define what success looks like for your CRM implementation:

- **Adoption Rates**: Track how many team members actively use the CRM.
- **Efficiency Gains**: Measure time saved or improvements in customer response times.
- **Revenue Impact**: Assess whether the CRM contributes to increased sales or customer retention.

Final Thoughts

A CRM isn't just a tool; it's an investment in your business's future. By carefully weighing costs against benefits, committing to thorough training, and fostering a culture of continuous improvement, you can ensure your CRM delivers maximum value. Remember, success comes not just from choosing the right software but also from empowering your team to use it to its fullest potential. If at any point the process becomes more than you can handle by yourself, reach out to the experts and leverage their expertise. Most CRM software solutions have certified consultants that you can hire to walk you through the entire process from Needs Analysis, to Design and Customization, through Implementation and Training. The best way to choose a professional is by the questions they ask. Take inventory of how well they get to know your business and what evidence of that analysis they put in your hands. Documentation is always a great gift after the consultant exits the stage. Make your selections based off of how well they listen and understand what you need.

Conclusion

A well-selected, properly implemented, and widely adopted CRM can transform your business. It's a tool that has the potential to enhance every aspect of customer interaction, streamline processes, and provide invaluable insights. But here's the reality check: <u>up to 90% of CRM implementations fail because of poor user adoption.</u>

Tangible Benefits of CRM Adoption

The numbers speak volumes about the value of CRM systems:

- Businesses utilizing CRM systems have seen a **29% increase in sales productivity** and a **34% boost in efficiency**, directly contributing to higher revenue.
- CRM adoption enhances customer retention rates by as much as **27%**, thanks to improved customer interactions and personalized service.

- For every dollar invested in a CRM, businesses can expect a return of up to **$45.72**, often achieved in six months or less.

On the flip side, companies without a CRM or with poor adoption lose **550 hours annually** due to inefficient processes like manual data entry. The comparison is stark: businesses with CRM systems thrive on streamlined workflows, while those without often grapple with inefficiencies.

Timeframe for Results

On average, companies begin to see positive results from CRM implementation within **3 to 6 months**. This time frame varies depending on the size of the business, the complexity of the system, and the level of user adoption and training. Investing in proper on-boarding and continuous learning significantly accelerates this process and maximizes the ROI.

Case Studies in CRM Success

1. **Small Retail Business**: A boutique clothing retailer implemented a CRM to manage customer preferences and communication. Within six months, they saw a **20% increase in repeat sales**, driven by targeted email campaigns and personalized offers.
2. **Professional Services Firm**: A consultancy firm adopted a CRM to streamline its client on-boarding process. By automating repetitive tasks, they saved **10 hours per week per consultant**, which allowed more time for client engagement and higher billable hours.
3. **E-commerce Start-Up**: Using a CRM integrated with

their e-commerce platform, a start-up tracked customer purchase behaviors. This insight resulted in a **15% boost in up-selling opportunities** and higher overall cart values.

The User-Centric Approach

When selecting a CRM, think beyond the bells and whistles. Ask yourself:

- **Is it intuitive?** Can users navigate it easily without constant support?
- **Does it integrate well with existing tools?** A CRM that complements your team's current workflows will see higher adoption rates.
- **Does it solve their pain points?** Identify challenges your team faces and ensure the CRM addresses them effectively.

A user-first mindset ensures your investment translates into higher adoption rates, higher revenue, and stronger customer relationships. The right system, combined with a team that's empowered and motivated to use it, becomes the difference between money lost and money earned.

Closing Thoughts

Adopting a CRM is not just a technological upgrade; it's a commitment to doing business better. Success hinges on aligning your CRM choice with your business goals and fostering a culture of engagement and learning within your team. With the right approach, a CRM is a strategic advantage that propels your business forward.

Implementing a CRM is more than adding new software—it's about embracing smarter, more efficient ways of working. Technology evolves rapidly, and businesses that fail to adapt risk falling behind. Leverage a CRM to maximize your team's time, talents, and efforts. Use it to create synergy, boost productive automation, reduce efforts and errors, and leave outdated practices behind.

The journey to greater success starts with a simple step: adopting a CRM that aligns with your vision and empowers your team. It's the first move toward a more dynamic, profitable, and future-ready business. Embrace the possibilities, and watch your business reach new heights.

www.ingramcontent.com/pod-product-compliance
Lightning Source LLC
Chambersburg PA
CBHW071111240526
45469CB00006BD/2438